Nighttime

Illustrated by John Butler

Written by Alastair Smith

Digital imaging by Keith Furnival

Designed by Verinder Bhachu
and Ruth Russell

Managing editor: Judy Tatchell
Managing designer: Ruth Russell

Owls

Owls hear the tiniest sounds. They can hear where things are, even if it's too dark to see.

This owl has caught a tasty rat to eat.

Owls live in quiet places. This is an old barn.

These owls are out to catch some food.

They sit quietly, listening for little animals moving in the dark.

Owls can turn their heads almost all the way around.

I can hear my dinner!

Moths and snails

Here's a moth, flying around looking for flowers that are open at night.

The moth drinks a sweet liquid, called nectar, from inside the flowers.

Take a look inside this flower.

Can you see
a trail of
silvery slime...

...and the snail
that made it?

Something has
made a hole
in this leaf.
Can you guess
what did it?

On a quiet
night, if you
find a snail
eating, you
might even hear
it munching.

Foxes

This fox is looking for
something to eat.

It's listening
quietly. Maybe
it's heard
something.

Young foxes
are called
cubs. Can you
find any?

Foxes live in dens under the ground. Can you find the way into this fox's den?

How many other nighttime animals can you see here?

Tarsiers

Tarsiers have very big eyes. They can see well in the dark.

They are small and shy. But it's easy for them to hide.

Tarsiers live in a part of the world where it is always warm.

What's this tarsier doing?

Tarsiers live together in groups.

Tarsier toes have sticky suckers on them. They grip tight to branches.

They hang on with their tails, too.

Mice

At night, mice scurry around. They hunt for food and bedding and things to nibble.

Mice have sharp teeth. They try to bite their way into just about anything.

People think that mice are pests. They chew things up and make a mess.

A mouse's teeth keep growing all the time, like your nails do.

Climbing is easy for mice. Their claws help them to grip.

They use their tails to hold on to things.

Mice gnaw things to keep their teeth short and sharp.

Fruit bats

In the hot, rainy forest, fruit bats are swooping around.

Look how the baby fruit bat clings to its mother as she flies.

Fruit bats are also called flying foxes. Their faces look a little foxy.

Whose little feet are these, sticking out through this chewed up leaf?

Cats

Cats like to go out at night. They hunt for small animals such as rats and mice.

What has this cat found?

Cats have soft paws, so they can creep quietly. Mice and rats can't hear them.

Cats are awake in the daytime too. But they do most of their hunting at night.

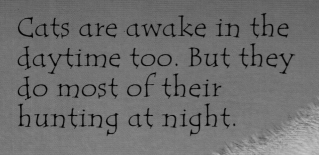

Cats can go in and out through a cat flap in the door.

Inside those soft paws are sharp claws. When a cat climbs a tree, it uses its claws to hold on.

First published in 2002 by Usborne Publishing Ltd, Usborne House, 83-85 Saffron Hill, London EC1N 8RT, England.
www.usborne.com
Copyright © Usborne Publishing Ltd, 2002.

Printed in Singapore.